Colorado ROCKIES

KENNY ABDO

Fly!
An Imprint of Abdo Zoom
abdobooks.com

abdobooks.com

Published by Abdo Zoom, a division of ABDO, P.O. Box 398166, Minneapolis, Minnesota 55439.

Printed in the United States of America, North Mankato, Minnesota.
102025
012026

Photo Credits: Alamy, AP Images, Bridgeman Images, Getty Images, Shutterstock
Production Contributors: Kenny Abdo, Jennie Forsberg, Grace Hansen
Design Contributors: Candice Keimig, Neil Klinepier

Library of Congress Control Number: 2025936779

Publisher's Cataloging-in-Publication Data

Names: Abdo, Kenny, author.
Title: Colorado Rockies / by Kenny Abdo
Description: Minneapolis, Minnesota : Abdo Zoom, 2026 | Series: MLB teams | Includes online resources and index.
Identifiers: ISBN 9798384940173 (lib. bdg.) | ISBN 9798384940937 (ebook) | ISBN 9798384941316 (read-to-me ebook)
Subjects: LCSH: Colorado Rockies (Baseball team)--Juvenile literature. | Baseball teams--Juvenile literature. | Professional sports--Juvenile literature. | Sports franchises--Juvenile literature. | Major League Baseball (Organization)--Juvenile literature.
Classification: DDC 796.357--dc23

Table of CONTENTS

ROCKIES

With a home field as high as their dreams, the Colorado Rockies always aim to be the best in the game!

COLORADO
1

The team's home-field advantage at Mile High Stadium helps the Colorado Rockies keep climbing each season.

BATTER UP!

The Colorado Rockies started in 1991 as a brand-new team in Major League Baseball (MLB). They were the first MLB team in Colorado. Fans across the Rocky Mountains were excited to cheer them on!

COLORADO ROCKIES

LINEUP CARD

DATE 4-5-93

	COLORADO ROCKIES		OPPONENTS N.Y. Mets
1	E. Young 2B	1	(S) COLEMAN LF
2	Cole CF	2	(S) FERNANDEZ SS
3	Bichette RF	3	(S) MURRAY 1B
4	Galarraga 1B	4	(S) BONILLA RF
5	Clark LF	5	(S) JOHNSON 3B
6	Hayes 3B	6	(L) ORSULAK CF
7	Girardi C	7	KENT 2B
8	Benavides SS	8	(S) HUNDLEY C
9	Nied	9	GOODEN P

EXTRA

LH	RH	LH	RH
Boston	Murphy		O'BRIEN
G. Young (S)	Tatum		BOGAR -
	Castilla		GALLAGHER
	Sheaffer	SWITCH	THOMPSON
		WALKER-HOUSIE	
		MCKNIGHT	

PITCHERS

LH	RH	LH	RH
Wayne	Blair	FRANCO	DRAPER
Henry	Smith		MADDUX
Aldred	Parrett		INNIS
Ruffin	Holmes		YOUNG
	Reed		
	Ashby		

The Rockies played their first game in 1993 against the Mets. Even though the team lost, the more than 53,000 fans were happy to cheer on their new baseball team.

In 1995, the Rockies made the playoffs for the first time as a **wild-card** team in the **National League** (**NL**) West. They lost to the Braves, but it was a big step for the young team.

GRAND SLAMS

The Rockies had ups and downs in the 1990s. Andrés Galarraga hit a three-run homer during a game with a 19-run inning. In 1996, Ellis Burks hit 40 home runs and stole 30 bases, joining just three other players in MLB history.

ROCKIES
Rocky Mountain News
Rocky Mountain News
Rocky Mountain News
WORLD SERIES 07
RED SOX ROCKIES
MOLSON CANADIAN
RED SOX
-VS-
ROCKIES
Coca-Cola
Coca-Cola

Todd Helton and Troy Tulowitzki helped lead the Rockies to some big moments. In October 2007, the team went on a “Rocktober” run, winning 21 of 22 games and making it to the World Series! They faced the Red Sox but lost in four games.

In 2018, the Rockies were one game away from their team **record** with 91 wins! They clinched the **NL wild-card** spot to make the playoffs. The team nearly won the **division** but lost a tiebreaker game to the Dodgers.

From 2019 to 2023, the Rockies had more losses than wins. However, in 2021, Trevor Story hit his 100th home run before leaving the team as a **free agent**. In 2022, Ezequiel Tovar made his **rookie** debut and stood out from the start.

ROCKIES

DOYLE

The Rockies struggled in 2024. However, Brenton Doyle won his second **Gold Glove** in a row. In June of the 2025 season, Hunter Goodman hit two home runs against the Marlins to end an eight-game losing streak. He was also named to his first **All-Star Game**. These moments proved there is still gold to mine in the Rockies!

HALL OF FAME

Todd Helton played his entire career with the Rockies. Known for his strong batting and steady defense, he won the batting title in 2000 and played in five **All-Star Games**. Helton finished with 2,519 hits and 369 home runs. He entered the Baseball Hall of Fame in 2024.

TODD LYNN HELTON
COLORADO, N.L. 1997-2013
ONE OF BASEBALL'S MOST EFFICIENT HITTERS WHO BLENDED PLATE DISCIPLINE WITH ELITE CONTACT SKILLS AND BRUTE STRENGTH DURING 17-YEAR CAREER AS FACE OF ROCKIES FRANCHISE. ACROSS FIVE CONSECUTIVE ALL-STAR SEASONS FROM 2000-04, LED THE MAJORS IN BATTING AVERAGE (.349), EXTRA BASE HITS (451) AND TOTAL BASES (1,832). HIS 2000 CAMPAIGN TOPPED LEADERBOARDS WITH 59 DOUBLES, 147 RBI, A .372 AVERAGE AND 1.162 OPS, AND WAS HIS FIRST OF BACK-TO-BACK SEASONS WITH MORE THAN 400 TOTAL BASES. LEFT-HANDER EARNED FOUR SILVER SLUGGER AWARDS AND THREE GOLD GLOVES, LEADING N.L. FIRST BASEMEN IN FIELDING PERCENTAGE SIX TIMES.
NATIONAL BASEBALL HALL OF FAME

Larry Walker played for the Rockies from 1995 to 2004. He won three batting titles and five **Gold Glove Awards** with the team. In 1997, he earned the **NL** MVP award. Walker became the first Rockies player to join the Baseball Hall of Fame when he was **inducted** in 2020.

Larry Walker
MVP
MEL OTT MEMORIAL AWARD
HOME RUN CHAMPIONSHIP

CARLOS
5 RF
GONZÁLEZ
HEIGHT: 6'1"
WEIGHT: 217
BATS/THROWS: L/L
BIRTHDATE: 10/17/85
BIRTHPLACE: MARACAIBO, VZ
ROCKIES
Coca-Cola
390
GONZÁLEZ
5

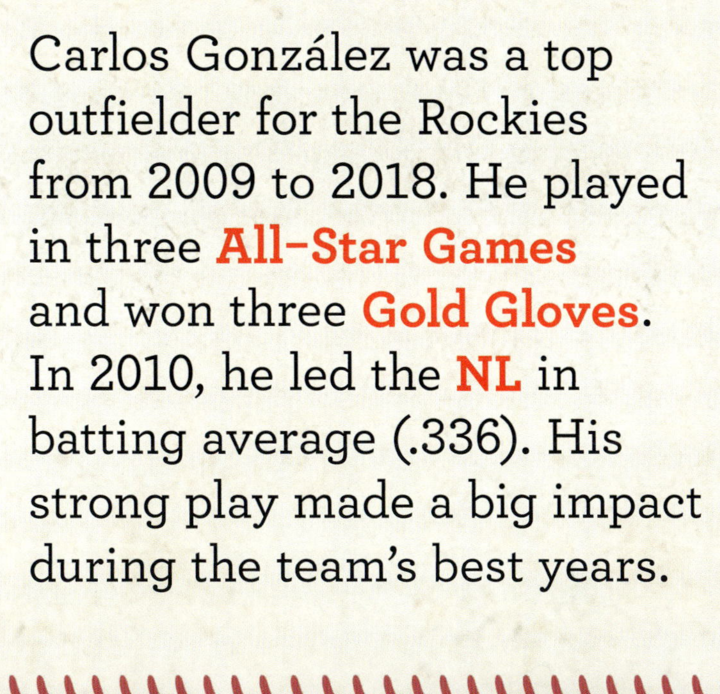

Carlos González was a top outfielder for the Rockies from 2009 to 2018. He played in three **All-Star Games** and won three **Gold Gloves**. In 2010, he led the **NL** in batting average (.336). His strong play made a big impact during the team's best years.

GLOSSARY

All-Star Game – a yearly baseball contest where top players from the American League (AL) and the NL compete against each other.

division – a number of teams grouped together in a sport for competitive purposes.

free agent – in baseball, a player whose contract has ended and who can now sign with any team.

Gold Glove Award – an annual award given to the best fielders at each position in both the AL and NL.

inducted – brought in as a member.

National League (NL) – one of two 15-team leagues that make up MLB.

record – a top achievement by a player or team that no one has done before.

rookie – a professional athlete in his or her first season in a sport.

wild-card – a place or a team chosen to fill a place in a competition after the regularly qualified players or teams have all been decided.

ONLINE RESOURCES

To learn more about the Colorado Rockies, please visit abdobooklinks.com or scan this QR code. These links are routinely monitored and updated to provide the most current information available.

INDEX